High-Performance Teamwork

by
Larry Meeker
Steve Fischer
Beth Michalak

photography by
J. Michael Blackwell

HRD Press, Inc.
22 Amherst Road
Amherst, Massachusetts 01002

Published by   HRD Press, Inc.
22 Amherst Road
Amherst, Massachusetts 01002
1-800-822-2801

First printing, October 1994

ISBN 0-87425-991-6

Production Services by Susan Kotzin
Editorial Services by Lisa Wood
Cover Design by Old Mill Graphics

TABLE OF CONTENTS

The Need for Teamwork!

The need is very real. Your company or organization needs solid teamwork to find creative solutions to today's business challenges.

Thousands of organizations are engaged in using some level of self-managed teams. Many organizations are finding teamwork to be important at all levels of the organization. This can include management teams, engineering and technical teams, service and support-group teams, as well as front line operational teams. Our businesses need actions by these teams, actions that *create improved business results.* The objective, therefore, of teaming programs is to achieve superior business results, such as improved quality, greater productivity, decreased cycle time, reduced cost, better product designs, more satisfied customers, and so on.

Many organizations are taking a great deal of time in developing and transitioning to teams. What we need are some tools to help translate the classroom learnings into actions. What we want are processes to take us from start up to achievement as quickly as possible. The goal is *effective teamwork.* This level of teamwork requires strong, effective relationships among members of our teams, in addition to the skills for working as a team.

This is, in fact, where experiential training plays a key role for *your* team. Experiential training will engage your team in exciting and entertaining exercises and events. These exercises are clearly defined physical and mental tasks that challenge the abilities of team members. By participating in these physical activities, you and your team gain a better understanding of just how you interact. Trained facilitators engage you in dialogue and assessment to highlight the team skills, interdependencies, and processes that your group employed to solve each challenge. This process, which combines hands-on experience with your teammates, followed by expert coaching and teaching is very powerful in bringing home important lessons. Through these experiences, you can get to the heart of vital issues such as trust, effective communications, the value of diversity, goal setting, and all of the other issues important to your team's effectiveness and success.

Experience is a very powerful teacher. In many cases, it is the *only* way to translate learning into skills and action. As a simple example, think for a moment about the process of learning to ride a bicycle. You can attend a class and learn a lot about how to ride a bicycle. Through careful study, you can become an expert in the dynamics involved, learning all about the mechanics between the machine and the rider. Safety and procedures can certainly be learned in the classroom setting.

But *how* do you really learn to ride that bicycle? How is that knowledge transitioned into successful action? Clearly, it is not until you get on that bicycle that you truly start to learn the skills involved in actually riding the bike. Experience is the key to actually performing the task.

This process of learning through experience is also a powerful way to learn many skills that are vital to successful teaming. An experiential training program also has the advantage of providing your team with an opportunity to explore and build relationships that are important to success.

Experiential training is very powerful. It can literally propel your teams forward in their development. This is even true for those that have been formed and established for a long period of time. If yours is a very experienced group, these training events can be used to revitalize members. These classes can act as something of a mirror for your team. You can see and assess how everyone works together, and work on ways to dramatically improve day-to-day interactions in the workplace.

The need is very real. Your organization needs rapid progress by your team toward excellent business results.

List some of the reasons why teamwork is important to your organization.

_____

_____

_____

_____

_____

_____

_____

_____

What are some actions/steps you can take to improve the effectiveness of teaming in your group?

_____

_____

_____

_____

_____

_____

_____

_____

Trust

*To trust someone makes a statement of faith
in them. It means you believe in them.
Relationships based on trust are vital to
high performance teamwork!*

Trust is a supremely important element in relation-ships between people. To trust someone makes a state-ment of faith about the other human being. It means you believe in the person, that you are willing to rely on his/her integrity, strength, ability and surety. It rings of confidence. Relationships strong in trust have a feeling and sense of security and strength. Strong relation-ships, based on trust, can be vital to your team's ability to achieve effective teamwork.

To build an effective team, you must have oppor-tunities to get to know each other and to establish trust. It is amazing how some teams plug along for years with members knowing very little about the personal inter-ests of those on their team. It is essential to recognize the tremendous value that exists in getting to know your teammates better. Learning about each other can set the stage for you to learn from each other. You will be able to draw from the strengths, knowledge, and experiences of these peers.

Trust can be a great enabler for your team. It will enable your team members to learn and succeed in many other issues and skills. It is vital to the effective-ness of your communications, your team's ability to make timely decisions, your success in solving prob-lems, your level of cooperation together, and your ability to proceed toward reaching the important busi-ness goals of your organization.

Trust and Empowerment

Empowerment is a major goal for many teams. As teams and people become more empowered, the effectiveness of your organization will grow. This process of increasing empowerment occurs over time. It is not an instant transition. The process of empowerment involves two parties, the person or team receiving increased empowerment and responsibility, and the person or group giving up some of their responsibility or authority. At the heart of this giving and receiving of empowerment is trust. It requires that the person who is giving up the responsibility trust those whose empowerment is increasing. It requires trustworthiness on the part of those receiving the empowerment. How does this trust and trustworthiness evolve? Well, it only grows and increases with time and experience.

Learning to trust each other during physical exercises and challenges can dramatically accelerate the rate of growth of trust on your teams, as it pertains to conducting the day-to-day business back in the workplace. Having relied on each other to be successful in a challenging learning event, and having relied on each other for physical safety during the exercise, goes a long way toward building effective team relationships that are based on trust.

High levels of trust between members of your team is a clear advantage. In fact, it is worth taking a moment to consider the seriousness of the alternative, not building team relationships based on trust. Unfortunately, lack of trust is quite damaging to relationships. Such a lack usually is far more serious than simply an absence of confidence between people. Instead, it often has far deeper consequences and can create very negative feelings, such as suspicion. Lack of trust can do more than just stop progress of a relationship or team. It can move results backward. It can prevent all hope of progress and success.

Investment in building trust on your teams has everything to gain. Ignoring this important component can be devastating.

Describe some specific actions/steps that can improve levels of trust on your team or in your department:

_____

_____

_____

_____

_____

_____

_____

_____

_____

_____

_____

_____

_____

_____

_____

_____

_____

_____

_____

_____

Effective
Communications

Open communications, within your team and with others, is a key to successful teamwork.

Communication: the imparting or interchange of thoughts, opinions, or information. Nothing is more central to the effectiveness of an organization than communication. It is a key to successful teamwork. Teams must freely interchange ideas and information, both within their team, and to the other people and groups around them.

This fundamental concept applies to any and all teams. It does not matter if it is an athletic team or a business team. How successful will a football team be if the players cannot clearly communicate, before and during each play, with the coaches on the sideline and with each other? Likewise, how much progress can a business team, or self-managed team, achieve without an effective flow of information with each other, to and from management, suppliers, customers, and others? Success truly is very dependent on this successful interchange of information.

When communications break down or fail, this can be very frustrating to the members of your team and can also be costly to the business. The frustration is to be expected. First, it is frustrating to miss a goal, or fail to meet a commitment. Then, the frustration is compounded, because you cannot understand the reasons for the failure of your communication. Your members may think they are doing a more than adequate job of communicating, but still they do not succeed.

Again, communication is the interchange of ideas and information. Effective communication, then, must mean that this interchange happens naturally and freely, throughout and across your organization. Success of the total organization is, in fact, very dependent on the capability of all of the people in the group to communicate.

What are some areas for improvement in your group's communications?

_____
_____
_____
_____
_____
_____
_____

What are some steps that you and your team can take to begin to improve communications with each other, and with the other departments in your organization?

_____
_____
_____
_____
_____
_____
_____
_____
_____
_____
_____

Team Spirit

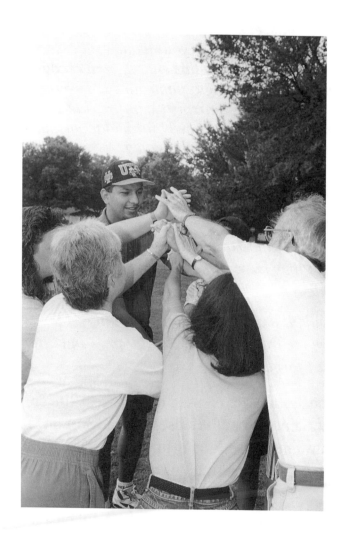

Recognizing and nurturing team spirit can provide tremendous leverage to accelerate teamwork.

The issue of team spirit as a business strategy is seldom acknowledged. However, when a collection of individuals gather and decide to form a team, a certain amount of energy is created. The harnessing and channeling of this energy into a positive force can be a powerful determinate for your team's success. Acknowledging the existence of this energy, and recognizing its influence, is of strategic importance. The recognition and nurturing of team spirit can provide tremendous leverage to accelerate newly formed teams, as well as mature teams that have plateaued.

"Sometimes it feels like a week of Mondays around our office."

"The only time that people ever talk to me is when they have something for me to do or I've made a mistake."

"Look, it's a job—it's not my family—they have me from 9:00 am to 5:00 pm—but after that I forget them."

The attitudes expressed in these real-life conversations certainly do not represent a platform on which to grow any enterprise. Yet, in business today, if you listen close enough, this attitude is nearing epidemic proportions.

In the legitimate pursuit of successful business, emphasis is placed on expedient outcomes. Those outcomes may be products, information, or service. In any case, outcome quality and delivery in an accelerated cycle is rewarded. Unfortunately, during the process in which these outcomes are developed, precious little time for any celebration is provided.

However, human nature often requires incremental affirmations of performance. The ability to develop team spirit provides a tremendous opportunity to assist your team in maintaining a positive environment. It is also beneficial to note that this spirit is contagious. Therefore, one individual on your team has the capacity to infuse energy into the entire group. Conversely, you have probably been exposed to the potential negative spiraling effect on a team, due to one member's poor spirit or bad attitude.

Three Principles of Team Spirit

First, spirit often begins with one individual and spreads contagiously. Someone who was previously either an anchor or neutral, in terms of emotion, can shift and become an energized leader. Any person on your team, without any organizational change, can become a leader or a coach, allowing the team to enjoy a special moment.

Second, during a normal business cycle, the inevitable frustrations, doldrums, and quieting points occur. To avoid a prolonged and sometimes fatal spiral into complacency, apathy, and ultimate failure, something must change. It could be something external and extremely significant, such as an increase in resources, or some technological breakthrough. However, more often than not, it requires the team members themselves to identify a way to revive themselves.

The third principle of team spirit is that it encourages the sense of "anything is possible." The sense of possibility can provide a tremendous uplift when your work team is faced with seemingly insurmountable barriers. The rallying of energies is often necessary to create an environment whereby elevated efforts are equal to or greater than the barriers. Team spirit provides a very real infusion of the "possible."

Team spirit is an emotion, and therefore your team must feel it. The positive outcomes of team spirit cannot be derived if they are only shared verbally, or written, and not experienced. It is important to remember that enthusiasm often ebbs and flows, but remember—you, or any member on the team, is capable of igniting, and sustaining, *"the spirit."*

List some examples of how your team or unit celebrates success:

_____

_____

_____

_____

_____

_____

_____

_____

_____

List some additional ideas for increasing team spirit on your team.

_____

_____

_____

_____

_____

_____

_____

_____

_____

Diversity

We have the most flexible, diverse society in the world. Your team's diversity, your differences one to another, can be a source of tremendous strength.

Many people in business give a great deal of credit for the "invention" of teaming concepts to corporations and organizations in foreign countries, specifically Japan. And, in truth, a number of important teaming concepts do have their roots there. Quality circles is certainly one example. It is interesting, however, that now that teaming concepts, particularly self-managed team concepts, are being embraced by many organizations in the United States, the capability of teams is much more powerful in the context of our country and our society. In this country we have the most flexible, diverse society in the world. Self-managed teams are proving to be an excellent vehicle for channeling our diversity, converting it into a powerful source of creativity. Empowering this creative energy through your teams is a fantastic way to promote new approaches to running your businesses more competitively. Teams that learn to value individual differences, and leverage them as strengths, tend to accomplish their goals.

Diversity is an important business issue today. It is a topic that is very high on the agenda for many organizations.

For some situations, a team simply cannot succeed without utilizing individual differences to their advantage. If your team learns this, it can be a turning point of maturity for the team.

This point of maturity can be very important to your team. Many teams, after formation, find some amount of migration of members into subsets of the team. Much of this is just a function of our culture and heritage. Sometimes these cliques form around race and culture. Sometimes the tendency is to collaborate by gender or age. Some differentiation can occur simply because of differences in personality. Some people are more humorous than others, some are more outspoken, some more quiet and reserved.

The sooner that your team learns that these differences are valuable, the better. These differences need to be recognized and utilized as strengths, rather than exist as points of division, or boundaries, that can have a negative impact on your team's performance. When your team values individual differences, the team will tend to make task and role assignments effectively. You will consider individual strengths and interests in allocating the work on the team. Members will be placed in assignments and roles where each is well suited to succeed.

Open recognition of the value of differences can also lead to some very exciting and fulfilling opportunities for individual growth and advancement on the team. It will be very satisfying to members who take on new challenges, and contribute to their company through the use of their personal skills and talents.

Your team's diversity, your differences one to another, can be a source of tremendous strength on your team. You absolutely cannot tolerate diversity being perceived as a weakness. This is an important challenge for all leaders and members in your organization.

For most people, their heritage and training has not done a particularly good job of making them, at the very least, comfortable with each other's differences. That heritage must be overcome. Experiential learning exercises provide the strongest tools to make that happen. Without training tools such as these, the time required to develop the appreciation for differences and diversity will simply take too long. ***Your organization needs the strength found in the diversity of your members. They need it now!***

Reflect on how you can enhance your team's performance by utilizing and leveraging the diversity of your team members:

_____

_____

_____

_____

_____

_____

_____

_____

_____

_____

_____

_____

_____

_____

_____

_____

_____

_____

_____

_____

_____

_____

Cooperation

Cooperation *will focus your team's energies and resources toward competing successfully in today's marketplaces.*

*"We have met the enemy and they are us." This timeless quotation often rings true within today's business environments. In an ever-increasing competitive global marketplace, the elevated preoccupation with competitiveness often causes organizations to implode. The drive for capturing market share, or bringing new products into the market, places a premium on organizations to nurture an infrastructure that optimizes their resources. If the climate within an organization is fostering a work ethic that encourages the "individual contributor mentality," little utilization of a synergistic leveraging of resources is able to occur. The outcome of that level of cooperation is **equal** to its parts, not the sum of its parts. That is not the desired result.*

Internal positioning and posturing detours necessary resources from focusing on the organization's business output. When the "enemy" becomes "us," valuable time and resources are often squandered. In place of the internal competition, more cooperation is needed to help organizations maximize the use of resources.

Cooperation is really a collection of more fundamental elements.

- A primary element to foster cooperation is that of a common goal. Owning the same goal and objectives can lead your team toward solid cooperation.

- In cultivating a cooperative culture, the element of trust is essential to your group.

- Cooperation among individuals, as well as among work groups, has a constant tension of give and take. Seldom is a cooperative relationship sustained for any duration when one party is constantly giving or taking. Work on balancing this tension within your own team, and the other individuals and teams with whom you interact.

- Effective communication skills become a pivotal determinant. It is hard to cooperate if information is not shared efficiently and equitably.

The outcomes of cooperation within work groups will continue to gain in value, as corporations move toward a faster paced global marketplace. The development of an internal cooperative atmosphere will help focus your team's and your organization's energies and resources *outward,* toward competing in the marketplace. No longer will the "enemy" be "us"!

Describe how you, together with the other members of your team, can create higher levels of cooperation and synergy:

_____

_____

_____

_____

_____

_____

_____

_____

_____

What might your team accomplish with more cooperation and cohesiveness?

_____

_____

_____

_____

_____

_____

_____

_____

_____

Problem Solving and Decision Making

Your team, if trained to solve problems and make good decisions, will be a source of creative solutions to business issues.

Part of running an effective business involves processes for solving problems and for making business-related decisions. Certainly, it is very important for your team, or teams, to develop skills in these areas, if they are going to increase their "ownership" in the operation of the business. The ability to make effective, timely decisions can be crucial to the success of any business. Your team, if trained to make good decisions, and when they are empowered to do so, can be the source of very creative solutions to business issues.

The level and quality of problem solving and decision making expected of your team today may be much different, and more demanding, than that expected of teams from just a few years ago. If your team today is expected to be involved in controlling and running the business, they cannot focus on single problems. That is just not the nature of running a business. In today's environment, your team must be able to tackle many problems, often simultaneously, to be effective in operating their piece of the organization's business.

Another important key to effective teamwork is the ability to make timely decisions. This is particularly important if your team is knowledge based, such as a team of designers or engineers. Recent research makes it very clear that teams who are capable of making timely decisions are much more effective than teams who struggle with decision points. Strong teams move rapidly through decisions, using flexible approaches to solving issues. Teams that do not tend to "tread water" much of the time, sometimes losing valuable days, weeks, or longer because they cannot reach even simple decisions. In most business settings, that loss of time can be very damaging.

One of the major advantages in using teams to solve business problems and make decisions is the formation of creative alternatives as solutions. Creativity, combined with the synergy of a team, can lead to fantastic innovation.

The challenge to your team's creativity in making decisions may exist in the boundaries imposed around the team. Some boundaries are real, some may simply be assumed. This is true even for mature teams, which have been intact for many years.

Another key to effective team decision making may rest in the team's willingness to use flexibility in their approach to making decisions and solving problems. When your team was first formed, the tendency may have been to use consensus processes for most, if not all, decisions. That can be valuable, particularly as team members learn to work together. As your team grows, however, taking every decision and issue to the entire team, expecting consensus, may not be very efficient. Flexibility in decision making based on the nature of the issue will keep decisions, and the team, moving forward.

The ability to solve business issues and problems as they occur is very important to your team's ability to succeed. Teams that are highly skilled in these areas spend less time "treading water," and more time moving their teams and their businesses forward.

List several important business decisions that your team currently faces:

_____

_____

_____

_____

_____

_____

_____

_____

_____

_____

How can your team optimize the solutions to these issues?

_____

_____

_____

_____

_____

_____

_____

_____

_____

_____

Quality of Life

*The impact of team training does not stop with
the team or business. It can literally help individuals
improve the "Quality" in their lives.*

The power of experiential training methods does not stop with the positive impact it has for your team and organization. This training can also have profound implications for the individuals on your team, at a very personal level. The experience can literally result in personal decisions and resolve to improve the quality of life of the individuals who participate.

The Total Person

A full life contains vital elements in the areas of social and emotional engagement with people, mental stimulation and growth, physical well-being and health, and spiritual growth and nurturing. All of these dimensions (social, mental, physical, and spiritual), are vital to your total health and well-being. Interestingly, all can be affected and enhanced through the experiential learning you complete as a team.

As your team members enhance their ability to work together with greater effectiveness, they are developing, on an individual as well as a team level, their ability to interact with people. This has important implications for their total lives, including the time away from the workplace.

This *social and emotional growth* can even have a big impact at the family level. A family, after all, is a very important team. "Family teams" are the fundamental building blocks of our communities.

Where there is learning, there is *mental stimulation and growth*. This is of fundamental importance to businesses. Learning, indeed, has implications at the personal level. The reaction to learning is generally quite positive. Broadening your own capabilities is usually a source of great personal pride and self-satisfaction.

The next important dimension is the area of *physical development and wellness.* When you feel well, and are physically fit, you perform better at everything you do. This not only includes work, but the infinite types of non-occupational and recreational activities that you may pursue. The important point here is that physical well-being is vital to the quality of your total life.

Everyone has a certain physical capacity. Some have physical limitations and challenges. Even so, your hardiness, within your individual capacity is of fundamental importance to the fullness of life that you will experience.

Finally, but certainly not least in importance, is the aspect of *spiritual renewal.* This is an area that is very personal and varied for different individuals. In the context of corporate experiential team training, the benefit in areas of spiritual renewal and development is the result of the inward reflection that occurs, as you see how you interact with your teammates.

Imagine what the potential of your team might be, if all of the people in your organization were to achieve very high levels of "Quality" in their lives. If your team has people who are healthy and physically fit, are mentally stimulated and continually learning, who suc-

cessfully engage with others, and feel spiritually satisfied, it will be a powerful team indeed.

Reflect for a few minutes on the relationship of the team training you are receiving and the application and impact it might have on your personal life. List some of the parallels.

_____

_____

_____

_____

_____

_____

_____

_____

_____

_____

_____

_____

_____

_____

_____

_____

_____

_____

_____

_____

_____

A Final Word

Experiential Team Building is about learning by doing, opening our eyes, and opening our minds to better solutions for today's business challenges.

The Urgency

Across industry, and in many other types of organizations, an urgency exists to run operations in a more efficient manner. Many organizational leaders have recognized that one of the keys to success, if not survival, is to get everyone in their organizations engaged in making the enterprise better. For many, teams have become the vehicle to get increased involvement.

In many organizations, layers of the organizational structure have been removed. This has been a reaction to reduce costs in the interest of making the organizations more competitive. In many cases, this reduction has been done somewhat surgically, without a redesign of the work processes that are in place. In other words, the amount of work remaining is the same, but there are fewer people to perform the tasks. Clearly, if your organization has been successful in implementing strong teams, teams who truly achieve effective teamwork together, it will have an advantage in facing these challenges.

Business Implications

Your team can hold tremendous potential for improving business performance for the organization.

In production settings, it is common for strong teams to rapidly accomplish significant improvements in quality, productivity, cycle time, and cost performance. All of these combine to improve the bottom-line cost performance of the operations.

With knowledge-based teams, improvement in the ability to make timely decisions, to solve problems effectively, to create innovations and products, are all enhanced through effective teaming. Being able to take innovative solutions and products to the marketplace, faster than the competition can be critical to the success, if not the survival, of your organization today.

Management teams are able to use their combined knowledge and abilities to create compelling visions for their organizations. It is their job to reduce the barriers that inhibit the performance of their business units, and the teams contained therein. There simply is no effective way to address these efficiently, without teaming together, tackling the challenges in unison.

Administrative and support teams are also vital in most contemporary organizations. Their challenge is often to continue, if not increase, and improve levels of support, often with fewer resources. Again, teams can be the key to timely success.

Virtually all disciplines within your organization stand to gain a great deal from strong performing teams.

Keep the Momentum Alive!

Teams, periodically, may need rejuvenating. They may fall into routines that result in plateaued levels of team performance. The membership of a team may shift and change with time. When new members fill the ranks of the team, relationships must be developed once again. Whatever the reason, even the most effective of teams needs an occasional breath of new life. As this occurs, you can use more experiential team building to accomplish this. You can go to a higher level of experiential learning, such as a high ropes course, or it may be as simple as some new initiatives, targeted at your current set of challenges and issues. In either case, it is a great way for your team to spring ahead in performance.

Teams make work more meaningful. The more high performing your team, the more meaningful the team and the work experience will be.

In addition to all of the business reasons to help your team become high performing, it is also important to remember the tremendous personal implications that result from strong teams. You and your teammates will achieve a great deal of satisfaction from being on a winning team. Enthusiastic teamwork that results in outstanding performance and winning is contagious. People want to be a part of it.

Experience is a very powerful teacher

Whether your team is new or well established the experience of doing things together can hold keys to achieving greater and greater team performance, performance that can be measured at the "bottom line" of your organization.

The experiential learning process is about learning by doing. Allow it to open your eyes, and your mind, to better solutions to the business challenges faced today by your team and organization.

High Performance Teamwork

Additional copies are available at the following prices:

1 - 10 copies	$5.95 per book
11-99 copies	$4.75 per book
100 plus copies	$3.75 per book

Name _____

Title _____

Organization _____

Address _____

City _____ State _____ Zip _____

Mail To : HRD Press , 22 Amherst , Massachusetts , 01002
1-800-822-2801   (Fax) 413-253-3490

Notes

Notes

Notes

Notes

Notes

Notes

Notes

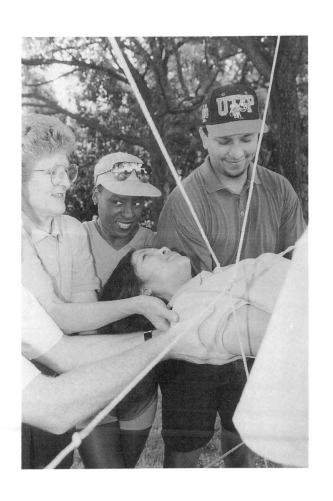